how2become.com

RAPID STUDY SKILLS FOR STUDENTS: HOW TO STUDY WITH DYSLEXIA POCKETBOOK

www.How2Become.com

rders: Please contact www.How2Become.com

BN: 9781912370146

irst published in 2018 by How2Become Ltd.

ypeset for How2Become Ltd by Gemma Butler.

Disclaimer

Contents

INTRODUCTION

For people with dyslexia, learning can feel like an uphill battle. While education on the subject and support for specific learning difficulties is at an all-time high, many students have still not have been taught some of the techniques that they can use to give themselves a helping hand.

Depending on the learning difficulty you may have, you will prefer to work in different ways. This is something that you may know already, or even be something that you still need to explore. Discovering how you work most comfortably is not always easy, so it is important that you take your time and experiment to find what works best.

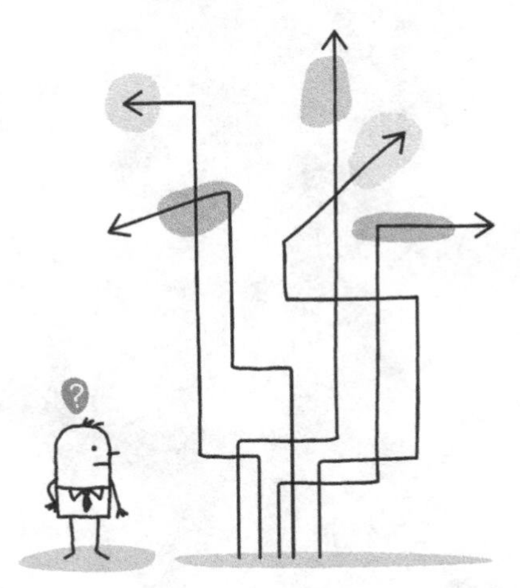

No matter what level of study you are at, from school to university, or if you're working towards any other qualifications, inside this book you'll find learning and revision methods that are best suited to how you learn, however that may be.

So, before we begin, let's talk a bit about a few types of learning difficulties and how they affect those who deal with them, starting with dyslexia.

WHAT IS DYSLEXIA?

'Dyslexia' is a specific learning difficulty that affects how people interact with words and numbers. For this reason, it can make studying difficult. Dyslexia can inhibit reading comprehension, and make people have to work extremely hard to understand what they're reading. It can also affect a student's writing. Again, dyslexics will usually have to work a lot harder to put sentences together than non-dyslexics. Despite this, dyslexia is not categorised as a disability because it has no relationship with intelligence.

This difficulty with reading and writing stems from the fact that dyslexia interferes with the ability to 'decode' words and sentences. This means that you may struggle to identify the relationship between the letters used to spell a word and the sounds that they represent.

Also, it may prove a challenge for you to 'break words down' and get to grips with why some words are formed and spelled the way they are. It may be difficult for people with dyslexia to become aware of word structure, and learn about word elements such as prefixes or suffixes.

Alongside these elements, dyslexic students may have difficulty dealing with text appearing on brightly-coloured paper, which may cause visual disturbances. To counter this, dyslexic students may benefit from placing colourful filters over their reading material in order to stop the words seeming to move around or vibrate. Despite this, recent studies have doubted claims that dyslexia interferes with vison in this way, suggesting that it is only a language-based condition. So, be careful of any miraculous products that claim to 'cure' dyslexia – just do what works best for you.

While struggles with reading and spelling are what everyone thinks of when they hear the word 'dyslexia', there is more to it than that; people with dyslexia may also be affected in many other ways. For example, you may have more difficulty understanding and following instructions, even verbally, or struggle to organise and plan assignments.

Also, when it comes to revising for exams, dyslexia can affect your ability to retain information you've learned due to the fact that it may inhibit short-term memory. Usually, however, long-term memory will not be affected, so revising in ways that you know work for you will still yield good results.

Aside from this, there may even be symptoms that affect other areas of life, such as one's spatial abilities. This could vary from having difficulty with sense of direction, or being slower when it comes to telling left from right. What's more, all of these aspects of dyslexia often combine to affect self-esteem, which is often lower among dyslexics than non-dyslexics.

Dyslexia affects people differently – symptoms can manifest themselves to varying degrees of severity or not appear at all. This can make dyslexia difficult to identify, as symptoms may go unnoticed or be written off as simply being a part of growing up.

Now, let's look at another specific learning difficulty – dyscalculia.

WHAT IS DYSCALCULIA?

Dyscalculia is a specific learning difficulty relating to mathematical concepts and numbers. For example, when faced with two different numbers, children with dyscalculia may struggle to identify which of the two is 'larger'. Somewhat similarly to dyslexia, people with dyscalculia may also struggle with short-term memory, and struggle to keep numbers in their head when doing sums. Also, dyscalculia may inhibit a child's ability to recognise the relationship between numbers and their corresponding written forms. For example, the relationship between '8' and 'eight'.

In older students and adults, dyscalculia will affect the ability to deal with graphs and charts, spreadsheets, or equations that have been spoken out loud. Also, dealing with finances will often require a concerted effort on the part of someone with dyscalculia. As well as this, it may make remembering dates and times difficult or confusing.

WHAT IS DYSPRAXIA?

Dyspraxia or 'DCD' (developmental coordination disorder), is a condition that affects physical movement. Like dyslexia and dyscalculia, symptoms first appear in childhood and last for life.

There are numerous possible effects of dyspraxia, which can appear in different combinations or not at all. For example, people with dyspraxia will often struggle with hand-eye coordination. This may cause problems when learning to write, due to potential difficulties with gripping a pen.

Due to the fact that dyspraxia impacts upon physical movement, it may also present problems with speech. Children with dyspraxia may not be able to enunciate as clearly as their classmates, or even struggle to control the volume or speed of their speech. For adults with dyspraxia, speech may be disorganised; they may need to repeat themselves or talk for a long while to properly convey what they want to.

Also, similarly to dyslexia, dyspraxia can present issues with short-term memory, meaning that people with dyspraxia need to expend huge amounts of effort to retain information. Of course, this will impact upon revision and essay assignments.

YOUR TIMETABLE

Organisation

As mentioned in the introduction, if you have a specific learning difficulty such as dyslexia or dyspraxia, you probably have to work harder than your classmates or coursemates to stay as organised as they do. However, there are specific actions you can take in this area to try to minimise the stress that your day-to-day schedule may be causing.

In essence, this means discovering the organisation techniques that work for you and using them as much as possible. This may even extend to your life outside education. Let's now discuss a few steps you can take to increase your general levels of organisation!

Timetable

Of course, this is an obvious place to start, but it's also the most important as it represents the foundation for many other methods of organisation. Each week, you should timetable as much as possible, noting down every class and study session you have in the coming days. As well as this, note down the time you plan to spend on homework or assignments. While it will be difficult to get this spot on every week, you will know how much time you generally spend on certain tasks.

- Colour-coding

Colour-coding your timetable is a great way to create mental links and make things stick when you revise. For day-to-day timetabling, however, it's extremely useful for creating an at-a-glance visual representation of how your time is divided up.

Once you've created your timetable, mark each subject or class with its own colour, and homework and study time in another. Once you're done, you'll be able to visualise your plan for the week much more efficiently.

You could also consider using the different colours to represent the difficulty of each of the subjects. Shade the subjects you're most comfortable with in green, and your least favourite ones in red.

- Time estimations

A key part of planning your timetable will be to estimate how long it takes you to perform certain tasks, so you can accurately plan your week. While it's impossible to get this exactly right every single time, you will know which tasks take longer than others. So, reflect this in your timetable – there's no need to plan in slots that are all the same length.

- Time of day

Another thing to consider when timetabling, is the time of day that you feel your productivity peaks. You may hate early mornings, and find that you study best in the evening, or the complete opposite could be true. So, make sure that this is reflected in your week-to-week timetable.

While you won't be able to change the times that classes, lectures, or seminars take place, you can with everything else! So, don't be too influenced by what others around you are doing. Choose a study time that works for you, and pick a time when you know that you'll be motivated.

- Environment

Think about where you currently do your studying. While you might not think it matters so much, your environment can have a large effect on your ability to take in and process the information that's in front of you.

Luckily, there are a few clear and easy steps you can take to ensure that your surroundings are helping, not hindering!

Light – If your surroundings are too dark, the muscles around your eyes will tire quicker than normal. Reading in too bright a light will be distracting, and could cause headaches or a loss of focus.

Posture – While favoured reading position will of course vary from person to person, everyone should consider a couple of questions. Do you study at a desk, sitting on a chair with good back support? Does studying in bed really allow you to get into 'work mode'?

Distractions – Think about if there is anything you should remove from your study environment in order to minimise distractions; save watching that show for your break! If you're really struggling, there are web browser plug-ins that disable potentially distracting websites. Alongside this, don't be afraid to tell the people around you that you need some space during study time.

Fresh air and breathing – Breathing techniques are beneficial to concentration and stress-relief, which are both vitally important throughout your studies. So, make sure that your study space has a plentiful supply of fresh air, which will ensure sufficient oxygen levels in your bloodstream. This will maintain your energy levels and keep your head clear.

- Reward yourself

Don't forget to include your downtime and rest breaks in your weekly timetable, as well as your extra-curricular commitments. Again, this will involve thinking about how long you can usually work for without needing a break. Having said this, there's no need to follow your planned breaktimes too rigorously. When carrying out your timetabled hours, you may feel you need more or fewer breaks – don't be too afraid of adjusting accordingly.

- Take action if it goes wrong

This is something very important to consider when timetabling and studying. Say you've finished creating your timetable for the week, and you're pleased with how it looks. But, when it comes to actually studying during the planned hours, you're struggling massively, and can't seem to meet what you've set for yourself.

This is the time to act – while it will be extremely annoying at first, quitting while you're ahead and creating a new, more realistic timetable will be a lot more beneficial for you moving forwards.

- Know yourself

You'll have noticed that a common theme throughout this section has been 'know yourself'. Your timetable must be very personal to you, and tuned to how you study. This is to ensure that your study time is as efficient as possible. Along these lines, there is another important way that you should know yourself.

As you may be familiar with, it is possible to talk about 'learning styles', namely 'Visual Learning', 'Aural Learning', and 'Kinaesthetic Learning'. These all deal with how people prefer to learn.

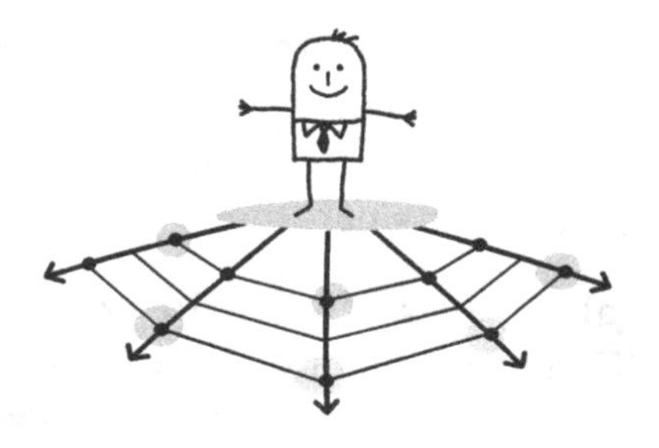

If you are someone who has dyslexia, then exploring different learning methods could be very useful for you.. Take our learning style quiz below to discover learning ideas that could suit you.

THE THREE TYPES OF LEARNER

There are three major ways that people revise and absorb information. These are:

Visual Learning – This involves using visual aids such as note-taking and creative mapping of information, to commit things to memory.

Kinaesthetic Learning – Using activities involving interaction to remember key details (such as flashcards and revision games).

Aural Learning – The use of videos, music or other recordings to allow information to sink in.

Different paths will work better for different people, but also bear in mind that certain subjects will also suit these methods differently. For example, Maths may be better suited to visual learning than aural learning, because mathematics (sums and equations) is more visually-oriented than other subjects. However, certain rules or formulae could be learned by placing notes around your study space, if you're a kinaesthetic learner.

Essentially, you will need to experiment with different styles in order to find which ones best suit you, but you will also need to discover which works best for what you're studying for. In the next three sections, we will examine the different methods of learning in more detail. Additionally, each method will be paired with the subjects and exams which best suit it, as well as how to identify which style matches your own.

The quickest way to figure out what kind of learner you are, is to think of what works best for you when trying to remember something. When someone needs to explain to you how to do something, what sinks in the best? Do you learn by watching others doing it first, or by listening to their explanation? Alternatively, you might learn best by giving it a try yourself. Use the following quick guide to figure out what kind of learner you might be:

Visual – You learn best by watching others or reading information. If you're learning a technique in a game, sport, or other activity, you would prefer to watch videos of others doing it, watching people do it in real-life, or by reading explanations. You might also learn from looking at images or diagrams.

Aural – Listening is your preferred style of learning. You would rather ask for and listen to directions rather than look at a map. If you were learning something new, you'd rather listen to an explanation and follow the instructions.

Kinaesthetic – You learn by doing things rather than just listening or reading. Rather than being told how to do something, you try to do it yourself. You prefer practical, energetic ways of learning as opposed to the traditional methods of reading, listening, and note-taking.

Learning Style Quiz

The following learning style quiz can be used to figure out which of the above learning styles suits you best. Once you're done, head to the answers section, where all will be revealed!

1. If you were watching an advertisement for a product on TV, how would you most likely react?

A) You'd notice the imagery, colours and other things happening on screen.

B) You'd recognise and listen to the music, and maybe even hum along if you knew it well enough.

C) You'd remember a time when you saw or interacted with the product in real life.

2. You're using a programme on your computer and can't figure out how to perform a specific task. How would you learn how to do it?

A) Watch an online video tutorial of someone doing it.

B) Ask someone to tell you how to do it.

C) Attempt it yourself until you figure out how it's done.

3. If you had to learn lines for a theatre production, how would you do it?

A) Sit down with the script and read your lines in your head.

B) Read the lines out loud to yourself.

C) Get together with a few other people and act out your scene(s).

4. You need to remember someone's postcode, so that you can find their house. How do you best remember it?

A) Visualise the letters and numbers.

B) Repeat the postcode out loud to yourself.

C) Write it down.

5. You're doing some fairly simple mental arithmetic. How would you solve the sum?

A) By visualising it in your head.

B) By saying the numbers and the operation out loud, step-by-step.

C) By counting or subtracting on your fingers, or by using objects nearby (such as counting pens and pencils).

6. Which of the following would you most likely do for fun?

A) Watch TV.

B) Listen to a radio show or podcast.

C) Play a video game.

7. You're queueing for a theme park ride and the wait time is quite long. Which of the following would you most notice whilst in the queue?

A) The decorations in the queueing areas.

B) The music or sound effects playing in the background.

C) How long it's been since you last moved in the queue.

8. If you saw the word "apple" written down, how would you react?

A) By visualising the word "apple" in your head.

B) By saying the word out loud to yourself.

C) By imagining things related to apples (cores, pips, trees, etc.).

9. You're in a new place for the first time and need directions. What would you do?

A) Find a map and follow it.

B) Ask someone for directions.

C) Keep walking around until you find the location for yourself.

10. When you meet a new person, what do you remember the most?

A) Their face.

B) Their name.

C) What you did with them, or what you talked about.

Now that you've finished, you can find out what kind of learner you are:

- If most of your answers were A, then you are a **visual learner**. You learn by using your eyes to analyse diagrams and notes.
- If most of your answers were B, then you are an **aural learner**. Spoken words sink in best, so you do well when listening to yourself or others.
- If most of your answers were C, then you are a **kinaesthetic learner**. You study best when getting involved and doing things for yourself, rather than watching or listening.

Remember that you don't necessarily have to fall into just one of these three categories. A wide range of learning methods might work for you, so it's good to keep experimenting to find out which techniques suit you best.

In the next few sections, we will cover the three main styles of learning, so you can get some top tips on how to study efficiently!

VISUAL LEARNING

Visual learning is exactly as it sounds – you learn by visually representing information, or by having information visually represented for you. This can involve pages of notes, mind maps, tables, animations, slideshows and more. All of these can be used to make information easy to digest visually.

While modern computers are adept at note-taking and mind-map making, you might find it more helpful to ditch the laptop for a while and use a pen and paper. This way, you can improve your handwriting skills, make notes which are available at any time, as well as avoid distractions which come too easily whilst on a computer connected to the internet!

Visual learning is excellent for any subject that has a lot of written text to digest, where a passage of information needs to be dissected to find the most important parts. Note-taking can condense a whole chapter of dates, facts and figures into a page or two. Mind maps are a great way of connecting loads of key facts to a single core concept, such as an event or an important person. Additionally, videos and slideshows are excellent for representing data in a clear manner.

Visual learners tend to be good at remembering images and charts. They'll likely find it easier to remember details of pictures and photographs, and might perform well in memory games where they have to spot which object has been removed from a collection. For this reason, visual learners are suited to organising their revision materials into diagrams, which they will likely find easy to remember.

Depending on what you're studying for, you'll have a huge amount of information that you need to retain for the exams, regardless of what subject you're revising. Some of the following visual learning techniques, such as note-taking and mind maps, are excellent for storing large amounts of information.

NOTE-TAKING AND SUMMARISATION

This method is exactly as it sounds: you write down notes based on the information in your textbooks or lesson materials. The goal is to collect all of the vital information from your resources.

Use the following steps to take notes effectively:

1. Read through your textbook and other learning materials once, without making notes. Do this so that you get an overall understanding of the material.
2. Go back to the start of the material and begin to re-write the key details in your own words. Alternatively, if the book belongs to you, you can underline key points.
3. Continue re-writing important details until you've finished a whole chapter. Make sure to organise the bullet points into sections.
4. Once finished, read over your notes.
5. Then, turn your pages of notes over so you can't see them, then try to remember as much as possible.
6. Repeat this until you're able to remember all of your notes without reading them.

How you go about writing these notes will depend on what you're studying and which techniques best suit you. One way to help notes stick in your head is to underline the key words from sentences in your text books or other materials. Once you've done that, you can lay them out in your notes. This is beneficial because it separates the important details from the less important ones. For example:

> *"One of the key themes of William Shakespeare's 'Othello' is jealousy. Iago warns Othello of jealousy being a "green-eyed monster," and ultimately it's Iago's exploitation of Othello's jealousy that leads to Othello's downfall."*

By underlining all of the key information, we can now organise the facts from the above paragraph into something easier to remember:

- *Key theme = jealousy.*
- *Iago warns Othello of a "green-eyed monster".*
- *Iago exploits Othello's jealousy.*
- *This results in Othello's downfall.*

This method allows you to organise information succinctly, so when you return to read it later, you can absorb the vital facts and leave everything else out. By limiting yourself to these facts, you can focus on the details which are necessary. This is useful because you don't want to overload your brain with long, clunky sentences when all you need is the important stuff. What's important is that you transfer the notes into an easily digestible format.

For longer pieces of text with more vital information, you may need to write notes in full sentences. This can be a great way to improve your handwriting and writing skills. The other beneficial part of this method comes in the form of re-writing the information in your own words. It may be tempting to fall into the habit of copying information word-for-word; you might even find yourself doing this without thinking about it. If you're doing this, you're probably not internalising the information, and you might not even understand it properly. There are plenty of machines capable of copying things exactly, but that doesn't mean that they understand the information that they're making copies of! So, you should prove that you understand what you're reading by turning it into your own words.

For example:

> *"One of the key themes of William Shakespeare's 'Othello' is jealousy. Iago warns Othello of jealousy being a "green-eyed monster," and ultimately it's Iago's exploitation of Othello's jealousy that leads to Othello's downfall."*

This could become:

> *"Jealousy is the main theme of 'Othello'. In the play, Iago warns Othello that jealousy is a "green-eyed monster". In the end, Iago takes advantage of Othello's jealous nature and this results in Othello's downfall."*

Here, the meaning of both texts remains largely the same. However, by writing the work in your own words, you are demonstrating to yourself that you have identified the key parts of the text and understood them. Writing information in your own words is a great way to test your comprehension of the text; if you're able to sum up the message of the paragraph in your own words, then you probably understand its content quite well.

Although writing notes allows you to read over them later, the key part of this process is writing them in the first place. When you turn notes from a text into your own writing, you're committing them to memory. Reading the notes afterwards may be helpful in the short-term, but actually writing them will help the information sink into your head. As a result, it is be more likely to become part of your long-term memory.

Visual learners also benefit from making their work more vibrant and striking. This can be done by using different text sizes or colours. For instance, you could write more important words in larger text so that they stand out more. So, when you return to read your notes, you'll see the vital details immediately.

> *"Jealousy is the main theme of 'Othello'. In the play, Iago warns Othello that jealousy is a "green-eyed monster". In the end, Iago takes advantage of Othello's jealous nature and this results in Othello's downfall."*

Different colours could represent different things in your work. For example, if you were given a text including the pros and cons of nuclear energy, you could highlight the positive parts in green and the negative parts in red. Then, you could use a colour such as amber (or orange) to show important details which aren't necessarily positive or negative.

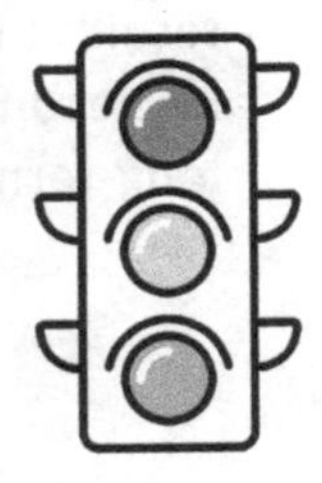

This traffic light system can be used in all sorts of ways. If you were reading a poem for English Literature, you might notice different themes. The main (most important) themes could be highlighted in green, less important themes can be highlighted in amber and then the least important themes could be highlighted in red.

Finally, you can write your notes as tables if it suits the topic. This is particularly useful for making note of 'for and against' parts of your course. For example, a student revising for Religious Studies might make use of the following:

EUTHANASIA: FOR OR AGAINST?

For	Against
It gives individuals the chance to die with dignity and relatively little suffering	The right to die might turn into the "duty" to die at a certain age to prevent strain on health services
Legal euthanasia treats individuals as sensible people with personal liberty	In some cases, the individual might not be in control of their mental faculties and might not understand the situation properly
Less terminally-ill people in hospitals will free-up resources for people who can be treated and/or cured	Potentially de-values human beings just because they are ill, might make society less willing to help the elderly and terminally-ill
Prevents a terminally-ill person from becoming an emotional strain on the entire family	One could argue that it's against God's will to end someone's life

Note-taking is a great technique for any kind of learner to make use of, but it's certainly most beneficial for visual learners. For some people, note-taking is the foundation for all of their revision, and they use other activities to simply break up huge chunks of writing notes over and over. It can certainly be monotonous, but it's a tried-and-tested method that lots of students have made use of.

NOTE-TAKING: PROS AND CONS

Pros	Cons
Simple and often effective	Can be a strain on the hands after long periods of writing
Doesn't require anything other than a pen, paper, and textbooks	Can be incredibly monotonous
Can be used to practise handwriting as well	
Leaves you with pages of notes that you can read more casually	
Re-writing information shows you understand it better	

MIND MAPS

Another great way of visually representing your notes, is by creating mind maps. These are webs of ideas and information connected to each other, to show how they are related. Generally, a central concept appears in the centre of a page, and then other details spread away from it. This is excellent for quickly jotting down all of the information you can remember, and then organising it into sections. Take a look at the example on pages 56 and 57.

MIND MAPS: PROS AND CONS

Pros	Cons
Can be made by hand or on a computer	Not effective for some subjects, such as Maths
Forces you to write incredibly concise notes, which is great for remembering	Has the potential to be less efficient and more time-consuming
Excellent for memory since you can visually recall the entire mind map in your head	Not necessarily an excellent method if you aren't particularly creative
Excellent for subjects with lots of connected events or concepts	
Allows you to be creative, which can alleviate some stress	
If done by hand, can be a great way of improving handwriting	

- The foundation of Othello and Desdemona's relationship is passion, not love
- Othello believes that love in marriage takes time to develop
- Desdemona's platonic love to Cassia is misinterpreted by Othello as sexual love

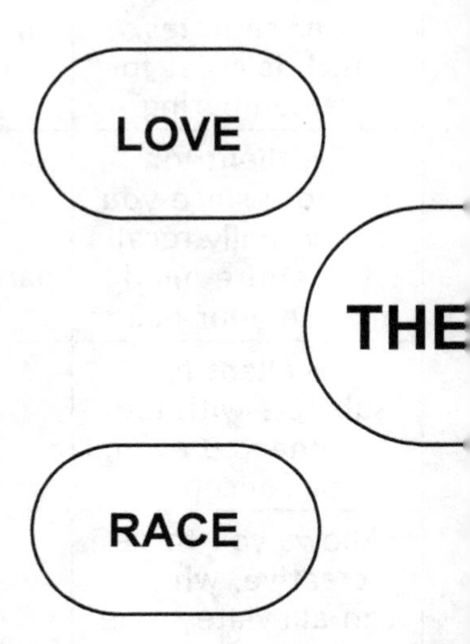

- Othello is black man in a high position in the Venetian military, which would have been unusual for the time
- Iago uses suspicions about Othello and Desdemona's mixed-race marriage to his advantage
- Othello has internalised some of this racial prejudice, believing himself to be unworth of Desdemona's love

- Desdemona's father sees Othello marrying Desdemona as theft of some kind of property
- The mixed-race marriage between Othello and Desdemona would've been unusual and likely the target of prejudice and scrutiny
- The two married women in the play (Dedemona and Emilia) are wrongfully accused of adultery

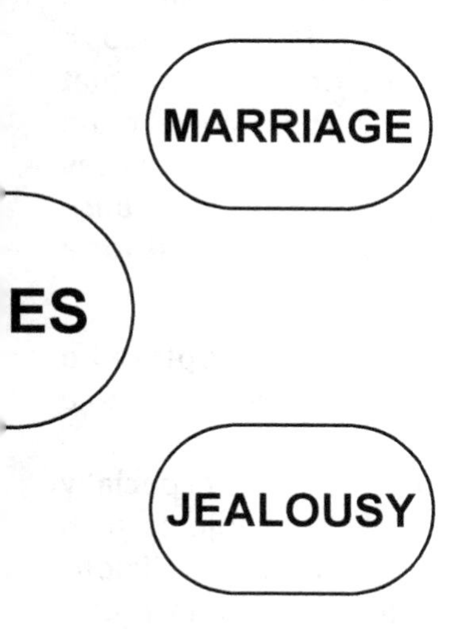

- Iago warns Othello of jealously being a "green-eyed monster"
- Iago himself has experienced jealously via his relationship with Emilia
- Othello's jealously clouds his judgement, despite him once being a calm and collected individual

VIDEOS, ANIMATIONS AND SLIDESHOWS

Visual learners can benefit greatly from watching videos and animations to help them revise. There's a wealth of videos online, often made by people who recently sat exams, which can be used to help you get a better grasp of the material. Head over to a popular video-sharing website such as YouTube and search for the topic you're currently revising. Always double-check that the information that they give is correct and relevant (by comparing what the videos say to what's in your own resources), because it's possible that these people studied for a different test than you.

Watching videos created by people who didn't write your textbooks is great for some subjects because it may offer alternative opinions and viewpoints. This is especially useful for essay-based school subjects such as English Literature, History, and Religious Studies, where having a range of interpretations and different opinions at your disposal can flesh out your answers even further. This is less important for other academic subjects such as the sciences or Maths, but nevertheless these videos still serve their function of being interesting to the eye.

Outside of the usual video-sharing sites, there are plenty of online resources which will give you videos, animations and slideshows to help you get your head around whatever you're currently revising. Again, remember to check that the information you're receiving matches what's in your textbooks.

This method is great for splitting up long sessions of note-taking. If you've spent the whole day revising, and you're getting tired of writing down notes, watching some revision videos online might provide some relief.

Note: watching videos online can be an excellent way of revising, but make sure that you stay on topic. It's far too easy to get distracted by everything else on the internet (e.g. social media, online games) – stay focused!

VISUAL AIDS: PROS AND CONS

Pros	Cons
Can be interesting or even funny to watch, and this can help ideas stick in your brain	Access to the internet can lead to easy distractions if you don't exercise self-restraint
Can give you an insight on alternative arguments and points of view	Sometimes the content in the videos won't completely match what you're being tested on – some things might not be relevant
Works as a good break from more intensive revision activities	

AM I A VISUAL LEARNER?

Do you find that you can recall information based on how it's displayed on a page? Try taking some notes or making a mind map based on resources in your textbooks, then turn the paper over and try and re-write the notes. Once you've re-written everything, flip the original page back over and see how well you did at remembering it all. If you could remember most or all of it, that probably means that you can learn from visual aids.

AURAL LEARNING

Aural learning is all about listening, both to your own voice and others. Aural learners absorb information by listening to it being said, either by themselves or by others. While it only really involves your ears, aural learning is incredibly flexible. There are plenty of ways to revise effectively if you are an aural learner.

Aural learning is excellent for subjects which have lots of short, sweet bits of information. For example, visual learners will likely write the process down as a series of bullet points, or perhaps a flow chart, whilst aural learners will want to listen to each of these points individually, to allow them to sink in.

READING OUT LOUD

This is the simplest method of aural learning, and can be done on your own and without any extra equipment. All you need is yourself, your textbook (or other study materials) and your voice!

Start by opening on a chapter or paragraph that you're comfortable with, and then begin to read it to yourself out loud. When you come across a sentence or point which might be more complicated or confusing, read it multiple times. By doing this, it will stick in your head more, making you more likely to remember it.

Aural learners can benefit from using certain tones for different points. Singing notes that you need to remember, or creating catchy rhymes for them, can help you to keep them in mind more easily. It might sound silly at first, but they can be incredibly useful.

Aural learners can create acrostics and mnemonics to help them remember difficult spellings or more complex ideas. Acrostics and mnemonics are almost opposites of one another. An acrostic is a phrase you keep in mind to remember lots of smaller phrases or information.

For example, BIDMAS is an acrostic which can be used to remember how you should go about solving maths questions:

Brackets

Indices (or 'powers of')

Division

Multiplication

Addition

Subtraction

Mnemonics, on the other hand, are a collection of words used to remember a single, larger word. These are particularly good for spellings:

BECAUSE =
Big **E**lephants **C**an't **A**lways **U**se **S**mall **E**xits

The colours in the rainbow can be remembered using the following mnemonic:

ROYGBIV =
Richard **O**f **Y**ork **G**ave **B**attle **I**n **V**ain

You can also use this acrostic to help you remember the colours of the rainbow!

Red

Orange

Yellow

Green

Blue

Indigo

Violet

Aural leaners can repeat the phrase "ROYGBIV" or "Richard of York gave battle in vain" until it sinks in fully. Then, if you got stuck in a test, all you'd need to do is recall the phrase!

Of course, the content at the level you're working at could be much more complicated than "ROYGBIV" or the spelling of "because". However, these exercises can still be used to remember key formulae and phrases.

Note: any kind of learner can make use of acrostics and mnemonics. Even if you aren't an aural learner, try them yourself!

READING OUT LOUD: PROS AND CONS

Pros	Cons
Requires very little equipment to get started	Requires a specific environment – a place where you're on your own and can speak out loud
Acrostics and other rhymes are bite-sized, meaning you can try remembering them on the go	Can eventually get tiring
Great for making sure you're actually reading the material and taking it in	
Has the potential for self-recording (see below)	

SELF-RECORDING

For this technique, all you need is your voice, some reading material and a device which you can record yourself with. In the past, you would have had to use a specific device called a dictation machine to record yourself. Nowadays, almost any modern smartphone or tablet has voice recording capabilities. So long as it has a microphone, it should be able to record your voice as well. If these options aren't available, dictation machines aren't too expensive, and they might be worth the investment.

Note: Many laptops can record your voice too. If it has a camera, it's probably capable of recording your voice with its microphone!

If you've chosen to use the "reading aloud" method of revision, you might as well record yourself at the same time. The self-recording technique is quite simple; all you need to do is record yourself reading your notes.

The great thing about this method is that both recording and listening help you to remember information. While you're reading your notes out loud into the microphone, you're going to be committing them to memory, just like you would when reading out loud. Once you're done reading all of them, you can listen to them through speakers or headphones whenever you're studying.

Here are some tips to make your recordings even easier to study from:

- Make sure you're not speaking too close to the microphone, or too far away from it. Do a couple of test runs to make sure your microphone is working properly.

- Speak slowly and clearly, so that you can listen back easily.
- Place emphasis on the more important details in your notes. Try changing your tone of voice for certain key phrases or facts, so that they stick out more.
- When you're done recording, send the files to your phone or smart device so that they're always handy.

Whenever you have a free 10 minutes or so, you can listen to your notes!

SELF-RECORDING: PROS AND CONS

Pros	Cons
Has all of the benefits of reading out loud	Requires some kind of recording device, might take a while to set up
Allows you to listen back to your recordings later on	

PODCASTS AND OTHER RECORDINGS

If you don't like hearing your own voice, or don't have a way to record yourself, there are still plenty of resources that you can listen to. Revision podcasts are easily accessible, and quite often free to download and listen to. There are also plenty of resources on YouTube (such as CareerVidz) and other video-sharing websites, which you can listen to via smartphones, computers, and tablets.

Remember to make sure that the revision materials are relevant. Depending on the exam board, the topics that you learn may differ. Before listening to a revision podcast, double check that the topics match those in your textbook or syllabus. If you're unsure of where to start, ask your teacher if they know of any resources that may be relevant.

Like self-recording, revision podcasts and other materials are useful because you can carry them with you at any time, with the help of smartphones and tablets. This means that, wherever you are, you can put a bit of time into listening to them.

Another bonus of these techniques is that they can be far less tiring. Reading out loud from a textbook or writing pages upon pages of notes can get incredibly boring, especially after long sessions. Using revision podcasts can often be a slightly more fun way of learning – so make use of it when you aren't feeling entirely up to more formal revision.

PODCASTS AND RECORDINGS: PROS AND CONS

Pros	Cons
Can be stored on a phone or mp3 player and listened to anywhere	Sometimes exact material in the podcast might not match your curriculum
Can offer alternative ideas and opinions which strengthen your own knowledge	Require some kind of device (e.g. smartphone, tablet, computer or mp3 player) to listen to them
Can be used as a break from doing your own revision	
Often free of charge	

DISCUSSING WITH OTHERS

Many revision techniques can be quite lonely. Sometimes, it's nice to have a bit of human interaction. Thankfully, aural learners can make use of discussion with a revision partner. This is a great revision method if you have a friend or family member available to help. All this involves is sitting (or standing!) with your revision partner and going through the material with them. There are two different ways in which you could do this:

- **Ask and answer questions.** With this method, your revision partner will hold the textbook in front of themselves for them to read, and then ask questions about the material. It's your job to answer them as accurately as possible. If you get the answer correct, congratulations! Move onto the next one. If you answer incorrectly, your revision partner can steer you in the right direction by revealing a bit more information, such as the first letter of the word, or some related details.

If your revision partner is taking the same test as you, then you should take turns asking and answering questions. By doing this, you're both being exposed to the material and can get things done quickly.

- **Open discussion.** This method involves you and your revision partner speaking freely about the material. If your partner is also studying for an exam, both of you should try to discuss without looking at your textbooks or notes. However, keep the books close by in case both of you can't remember something, or are unsure of precise details. It's also a good idea to share notes too, so that you can make sure that you've got something correct.

If your revision partner isn't studying for the exam (such as a family member), allow them to have the book open in front of them, but so that you can't see it. Then, just speak to them about the things that you're revising, and they can fact-check you along the way.

Both of these methods are great ways to learn with a partner, and are excellent ways of making sure that your other revision techniques are working. Discussing with a partner is most beneficial later on during revision, when you've already learned lots of information by yourself, and just want to test your ability to remember it.

Note: Thanks to modern phones and internet, you don't even need to sit in the same room as your revision partner in order to revise. There are plenty of communication apps and programs that you can download to your phone, tablet or computer which will let you revise with friends.

DISCUSSING WITH OTHERS: PROS AND CONS

Pros	Cons
It's a fantastic way of remembering information, as well as finding out what you know and where you need to improve	Can be difficult to organise, particularly outside of school hours
Benefits two people (you and your revision partner)	It's possible to get distracted and chat about irrelevant things!
It's a great way for friends and family members to get involved in the revision process	

AM I AN AURAL LEARNER?

Aural learners tend to focus on what they are hearing and saying more than what they are seeing and doing. If you think this applies to you, give some of the above styles a try. Aural learning is especially useful for those who struggle to sit down and take notes for longer periods of time, and the above techniques can be used by anyone who wants to mix up their revision.

KINAESTHETIC LEARNING

Kinaesthetic learning is all about *doing*, rather than looking or hearing. Kinaesthetic learners shouldn't limit themselves to sitting in one place and trying to write pages full of notes. Instead, they should be finding more creative and unconventional ways of learning. There's a huge range of techniques for a kinaesthetic learner to tap into!

Since kinaesthetic learning is such a broad field, it can apply to almost any subject and any kind of information. If you think you might be a kinaesthetic learner, give some of the following techniques a try.

FLASHCARDS

With flashcards, you'll want to write down some key notes from your textbooks or other revision materials. Take a large piece of card and cut it up into smaller segments. On one side of each card, write down the word or concept that you need to remember the meaning of. On the other, write down the key facts associated with the word. Here's an example to get you started:

Front	Reverse
Sonnet	A fourteen-line poem which is written in iambic pentameter. Uses specific rhyme scheme. Has a single, focused theme.

Once you've written all of your flashcards, turn them all facing front up and sort them into a deck (like a deck of playing cards). Then, take each card, read out the main word on the front, and then try and recall as many of the key facts as possible. You can do this by reading out loud, or by reading in your head – whichever suits you best.

Once you think you've finished listing them all, flip the card over to see if you missed any details. If you didn't, congratulations! Put the card to one side and save it for later. If you missed anything, take note of it and put the card back at the bottom of the deck. This means that, once you've got through all of the other cards, you can attempt the ones you couldn't completely remember before. One by one, you'll start to eliminate cards from the deck, since you'll remember all of the details for each of them. Once you've completed them all, take a short break before trying again.

Another method for using cards is to stick them around your workspace. Write a note on each piece of card and leave it somewhere in your room where you're likely to see it often. Stick some to your mirror or the edge of a laptop screen, or even place them on the wall or on a bookshelf. You can even leave them around your house so that whenever you stop to make yourself a snack or go to the toilet, you'll still be revising!

FLASH CARDS: PROS AND CONS

Pros	Cons
A pack of small cards is portable, so flashcards can be used wherever you are	Can take a while to put together (writing on individual cards, etc.)
They're incredibly useful for learning key terms and their meanings	
Writing them in the first place helps commit ideas to memory	

MULTI-TASKING

Multi-tasking simply involves doing another activity whilst doing your ordinary revision. By doing this, you'll start to associate certain facts with the things you do. If you enjoy exercise, try listening to recordings of yourself reading out notes, while going for a run or working out in some other way. If you play video games, stop and test yourself on a question every so often. This probably won't work as a main revision technique, but it's a way to do some light revision on a day off, or once you've finished the bulk of your studying for the evening.

MULTITASKING: PROS AND CONS

Pros	Cons
More light-hearted than intense revision sessions	Doesn't really work as a main revision technique
Can be done anywhere and at any time	
Bite-sized but effective	

LEARNING GAMES

For this technique, you're probably going to need access to either the internet or dedicated workbooks. You'll want to find games or other interactive tools which involve *doing* things rather than just reading them. For example, one game might require you to match up key words to their meanings, or key dates to the events which occurred on them. You can actually do this one yourself, in the same way that you made flashcards. Cut up a large piece of paper in separate pieces, and then on half of them write a key word. Then write something related to each key word on all of the other pieces. Shuffle up all of the cards, then try to match them up.

You should also check online for other learning games. As always, double check that the content of the games matches that of whatever you're working on, so you don't confuse yourself.

LEARNING GAMES: PROS AND CONS

Pros	Cons
Entertaining and highly effective for kinaesthetic learners	Online learning games aren't always easy to find
Works as a great break from more intensive revision methods	Creating your own learning games can be time-consuming
Can be an excellent way to revise with others	

AM I A KINAESTHETIC LEARNER?

If you find yourself *doing* things rather than reading or listening, then kinaesthetic learning might be the style for you. You might find that it's much easier for you to do something for yourself, rather than ask someone to explain it to you. You might also find that you work best in unconventional settings: maybe you work better while exercising than sitting at a desk.

LOOKING BACK ON YOUR EARLIER STUDIES

In previous books in this series, we've pointed out that GCSEs and A-Levels are great testing grounds for revision styles and techniques. If you've already studied for exams in the past, you can use this experience to your advantage. While different areas and levels of study will differ greatly in terms of content and difficulty, you can still learn from previous experiences with exams and revision in your life. Consider the following:

- What revision techniques worked best for you in previous exams and assessments? How can you apply them effectively to what you're currently studying?
- What didn't work so well? Is it worth giving it another try?
- What exams went well? Were there any tactics you employed during them that might've helped?

- What exams didn't go so well? What can you learn from your mistakes?

Feel free to experiment with learning styles and revision techniques, but don't be afraid to go back to what suits you best. Sometimes, being in your comfort zone is just what you need in order to perform well.

A FINAL WORD ABOUT LEARNING STYLES

The techniques explored here are only a few of the many ways you can learn and revise effectively. Start by experimenting with the methods we've listed, but feel free to branch out and try your own ways of revising. Different people think and work differently to one another, and so you need to find your own unique way of learning. Remember that, just because you may believe that you have a specific learning style, you don't have to stick to a limited range of techniques.

READING, RESEARCHING, AND REVISING

If you have dyslexia, then there are many methods that you can employ to assist your reading, with considerations to make before you start a reading task, during a reading task, and indeed afterwards. So, let's get straight into discussing what you should do before you go about reading something for your studies.

BEFORE YOU START READING

- Make a plan

If you've been set a reading task, or you need to research something specific for an assignment, you may not think that you can make much of a plan beyond 'read the content'. However, this is not the case. The plan you really need to make should be focused on minimising the amount you're reading, i.e. simply avoiding what you don't need to be reading.

So, before you start reading specific sections of a piece of text, you need to look at it as a whole in order to get a sense of how useful it will be for your task.

For example, say you are writing an essay on the role of Trotsky in the Red Army's victory over the White Army in the Russian Civil War. To research, you are reading a textbook on the Russian Civil War.

Your first step should be to read the contents page carefully; it will give you lots of information. Depending on how well you know the subject, you may need to read an overview of the Civil War to nail down other key figures, dates, and events. Contents pages are also a good place to get a sense on the author's attitude on people and events. Look for a sense of progression throughout the chapter names – you may be able to tell which side of certain debates the author stands on without having trawled through thousands of words.

However, the main goal of looking at the contents pages are to find the sections on Trotsky. In doing so, you will have immediately ruled out many irrelevant sections that you do not need to spend time getting through.

- Realistic goals

As touched upon earlier, you need to ascertain how long you can read academic texts for whilst maintaining maximum comprehension. This will vary from subject to subject, so you need to set realistic goals with each piece of reading you set out to do. This will be easier if you have timetabled well – you'll have anticipated the tasks that take longer.

However, this will be an ongoing process. Continuing with the Trotsky example, once you have found relevant reading material about Trotsky, you will need to set more specific goals within the general goals you have set for yourself in your timetable. Don't be afraid to take regular breaks to help maintain focus.

You may find that dipping in and out of texts and taking the 'little and often' approach brings about the best results. This is absolutely fine!

DYSLEXIA-FRIENDLY FONT

Something to consider is the use of 'dyslexia-friendly' font, some of which are in the public domain and freely downloadable. The way they work is by making each letter look completely unique in shape and slant, in an attempt to minimise the chance of confusing them. This involves making their shapes different lengths and widths. Also, letters are presented to be thinner at the top and thicker at the bottom, as well as to be further apart within words.

While there is no conclusive research into such fonts, many people have spoken anecdotally about how they have helped to ease some common reading problems associated with dyslexia. However, this may not work for everyone.

Below we have provided a piece of text written in a font called 'OpenDyslexic' (available from http://dyslexicfonts.com), just to see if it helps you in any way.

Extract from 'The Adventures of Sherlock Holmes', by Arthur Conan Doyle, 1892

We were seated at breakfast one morning, my wife and I, when the maid brought in a telegram. It was from Sherlock Holmes and ran in this way:

"Have you a couple of days to spare? Have just been wired for from the west of England in connection with Boscombe Valley tragedy. Shall be glad if you will come with me. Air and scenery perfect. Leave Paddington by the 11:15."

"What do you say, dear?" said my wife, looking across at me. "Will you go?"

"I really don't know what to say. I have a fairly long list at present."

"Oh, Anstruther would do your work for you. You have been looking a little pale lately. I think that the change would do you good, and you are always so interested in Mr. Sherlock Holmes' cases."

"I should be ungrateful if I were not, seeing what I gained through one of them," I answered. "But if I am to go, I must pack at once, for I have only half an hour."

My experience of camp life in Afghanistan had at least had the effect of making me a prompt and ready traveller. My wants were few and simple, so that in less than the time stated I was in a cab with my valise, rattling away to Paddington Station. Sherlock Holmes was pacing up and down the platform, his tall, gaunt figure made even gaunter and taller by his long grey travelling-cloak and close-fitting cloth cap.

How did you find reading this font? If it helped at all, it is freely downloadable on the website mentioned before the extract. You can install it to word and convert your reading material from the default font to the new one. You may even want to try writing in it.

TECHNOLOGICAL OPTIONS

Of course, thanks to the digital age we live in, there are lots of options when it comes to technological assistance with reading, writing, and planning. Focusing on reading, there is lots of text-to-speech software easily available online if you find listening to your notes easier than taking in the written word.

Similarly, the recent rise of audiobooks means that many of your set texts or articles that you need to know may be available to download in audiobook form. You can also find mind-mapping software, which can help organise your thoughts and save you time.

WRITING ASSIGNMENTS

Now we've covered techniques to do with reading, it's time to turn our attention to writing. In terms of assignments, read on for a 10-step checklist you should follow when completing essays and other written work. It aims to minimise the amount of time-wasting and stress as possible!

- **STEP 1 – Writing down ideas**

Before collecting your research or making notes, it's time to get your initial thoughts about the question out in the open. While the amount of personal opinion that is required for a task will depend greatly on the brief you have been given, this is still a worthwhile exercise.

The first thing you should do is start writing down whatever comes to your mind in no particular order – things related to the question, of course! There will be time to organise these thoughts later, so don't worry about making them too coherent or tidy. Just get your thoughts on paper or typed up.

- **STEP 2 – Write a rough plan**

Now's the time to organise the thoughts you've made into a rough plan. This won't be the final plan that you follow for the entire project – just a loose one to help you gather your thoughts for the research stage.

If you're writing an essay, try to construct a paragraph-by-paragraph plan in this stage. At the very least, you should have a good idea of what the sections of the essay or project are, and how they link together

- **STEP 3 – Gather and conduct research**

In this stage, you'll spend most of your time reading, working with others, or doing practical work so that you have something to support your assignment with. The exact nature of the research will depend on the subject and module that your assignment is in.

- **STEP 4 – Create a fleshed-out plan based on research**

Once you've got all of your research together, you now need to apply it to your plan. If you're writing an essay, you want to look for anywhere in your plan where you've made some kind of claim. Add relevant evidence from your sources here, so that everything you're going to write in your essay is supported.

If you're doing some other kind of assignment, such as a write-up based on lab work, your entire piece will centre around your research. Again, include evidence from your own research to your plan where relevant, so your argument is well-supported.

To make things easier, try to make a note of all the page numbers and locations of everything you're citing in your work. This will save you from having to trawl through all your sources looking for the exact line and page where you got your evidence from.

- **STEP 5 – Write the Assignment (First Draft)**

Now that you've got a full and fleshed-out plan, it's time to write the first draft. If you've taken your planning seriously, you shouldn't need to refer to any of your sources here – just follow each point of your plan, turning the bullet points and other short notes into full sentences.

If you've already made a full plan, this stage shouldn't take long at all. The key is to follow your plan as much as possible, and turn a series of notes into a coherent, eloquent piece of writing.

- **STEP 6 – Proofread the First Draft**

With a first draft finished, you should now read through it at least once. At this stage, keep an eye out for spelling, grammar, and punctuation errors – you don't want your work to contain any mistakes you could spot the second-time around.

Here, you can also get an idea of how your work flows from point to point. If you think some bits don't work properly, or something doesn't fit, make a note of it and then you can find a solution when you write the second draft.

- **STEP 7 – Write the Second Draft**

Writing the second draft is less a case of re-writing your whole assignment, and more of looking at the entire piece critically and trying to re-write parts so that they're even more concise. You might feel as though this is unnecessary, but going through and rewording things can help with clarity.

- **STEP 8 – Proofread the Second Draft**

As with the first draft, it's important to re-read your work to make sure there are as few errors you can catch as possible. You may also want to ask someone you trust to help you out at this stage to get their opinion on grammar and punctuation.

- **STEP 9 – Complete Referencing and Formatting**

Hopefully, you've been referencing as you go along. If so, there should be little to do in this section when it comes to referencing. Just make sure that you've followed the referencing system that your university and department have specified, such as the Harvard Referencing System. You will probably also need to write a bibliography – do this at this stage.

In addition, you should make sure that the formatting of your work meets the specifications of the department. If your work is word-processed, they might specifically request certain fonts, font sizes, and line spacing. Check the guidelines set by your department since some universities will dock points from assignments that aren't formatted correctly.

- **STEP 10 – Proofread and Check for Plagiarism**

In this final stage, you want to proofread your work and specifically check for plagiarism. Ensure that whenever you've used supporting evidence from a source, you've cited them properly. The aim of this is to make sure that you aren't passing off someone else's work as your own.

One way to check for plagiarism is to copy and paste sections of your own writing into a search engine. If this leads to results of places where you might have gathered ideas from, then you need to cite it as a source or remove the suspicious piece of text from your work. If you do remove it, make sure to replace it with your own work.

Of course, plagiarism is taken very seriously, so take no risks at this stage.

- FINALLY – Submit Work and Wait for Feedback

Once you get to this stage, you're basically finished. However, you still need to submit your work. Different universities, departments, and even modules might specify how to hand in your work once it's finished. Some might request a printed copy, whilst others will use an automated system where you can upload your work. In some cases, they might request both. Your department should make their requirements clear either on their website, or in the introductory documents for the course or module.

Once your work has been submitted, you'll need to wait for it to be marked. Hopefully this won't take too long, but different universities have different standards when it comes to turnaround on assessed work.

When your work and marks are returned to you, spend some time re-reading your assignment to see where you picked up marks, and where you lost them. Hopefully, the examiner has offered some feedback alongside the marked piece of work. Make sure that you read this feedback carefully and take it on board for your next assignment. If you don't get any feedback on your work, or have any questions, get in touch with your seminar leader or lecturer.

- Extra note-taking tip – Don't forget to mind the GAP!

Sadly, this doesn't involve an exciting trip to London; it's a simple acronym you can use to keep your note taking focused. It's particularly relevant for creative writing, and should serve to guide any research you're carrying out in preparation for embarking on your project.

> **G**enre – When taking notes before your project, know the rules surrounding whatever you're about to write. For example, if it's an academic essay, it needs to be in a fairly formal tone, with logical arguments made backed up with evidence. If it's a science report, you need to include an adequate conclusion or correct formulas. If it's a short story, you will need to consider the literal genre of whatever you plan to write!

Audience – Again, it is important to be mindful of who will be reading what you're about to write. Generally, this will be your teacher or tutor, so think about what they want from your writing. Most likely, this will be related to a mark scheme or assessment objectives. So, make sure you are familiar as possible with these and get your hands on them if you can. This will help keep your note-taking as focused as possible and cut down on wasted time!

Purpose – Similarly, during your research stages, you need to have a clear view of what you're hoping to achieve with your work. Again, this is how you will be able to carry out productive and relevant note taking. Once you know this, you can examine works which have achieved the same or similar effects. Thorough analysis like this will pay off – knowledge of how academic writers or past students have achieved good work in the same task will be hugely beneficial.

- Paper or keyboard

Now to think about writing a bit more generally. Consider the conditions around you when you feel most comfortable writing. A key factor in this regard will be whether you are writing by hand or typing on a computer or laptop. Only you will know which one you prefer, so maximise the amount of time you spend with your preferred choice.

- Technology

Taking notes, you may find it more convenient to dictate them, and have specialist software convert your speech into text. This way, you can put your ideas to paper while minimising the amount of writing you're doing.

EXAMS

Exams can be difficult, and you need to prepare for them in two different ways. First, you need to know the content of the exam. This is the actual information that you are going to be tested on – the stuff you've been learning in class, or on your course.

The second thing you need to learn is how to answer exam questions, and how to perform well in exams. This might sound strange, but a significant part of doing well in exams comes down to your familiarity with them, not just how well you know your subjects.

PRACTISE HANDWRITING BEFOREHAND

If your exams are handwritten, you need to make sure that your handwriting is legible. In the exam room, people tend to write incredibly quickly. As the exam goes on, some students will write more frantically, while others might slowly ease into the exam and get better as time goes on. Either way, ensure that your handwriting is as easy to read as possible.

In the exam, make sure to take your time if you feel as though your handwriting is suffering. If it helps, ditch cursive (joined-up) handwriting so that the words are easier to read.

Finally, you want to practise handwriting so that your muscles are used to writing for extended periods of time. This is important for avoiding hand cramp. Find a way of gripping the pen which is as comfortable as possible, whilst also being able to write efficiently and neatly. Learning some exercises to gently warm up your hands before the exam can also be helpful, and will hopefully make you less worried about your hands giving up halfway through.

If your assessments are based on the computer, you obviously don't need to worry about handwriting. However, if you need to type out your answers, take some time to work on your typing so that you can answer questions quickly and with no typing errors. Being able to touch-type is preferable, but not necessary – just make sure that you can type at a decent pace and with a high level of accuracy.

KEEP CALM

Getting a handle on your nerves can be really difficult during exam season, but remember that this is completely normal. If you consider that doing well in your exams is very important, then it would be bizarre for you not to be at least a bit nervous. Millions of people will be going through the same thing as you, and millions more have been in your position and have made it out of the other end in one piece. Life goes on after your exam, even if it doesn't feel like that during the heat of the moment.

Exams are stressful, and the conditions you take them in aren't pleasant either. Being stuck in a silent room for an hour, with nothing but a question paper and your own thoughts, can be incredibly daunting.

However, you need to remember that you're not the only one who feels this way, and that a bit of nerves can give you the boost you need in the exam hall.

That said, you need to keep any anxiety under control. A breakdown just before the exam (or even worse, during it) is uncommon, but just remember that not doing as well as you'd hoped in a single exam isn't the end of the world.

You might feel as though you aren't prepared enough, or perhaps a classmate or colleague has made you unsure about what you've revised – minutes before entering the exam room. This happens often, and can be incredibly demoralising. Remember that how prepared you think you are doesn't necessarily represent how well prepared you actually are. Sometimes, people who feel poorly prepared for some exams in the minutes before taking it end up doing incredibly well, and some people find themselves doing worse in exams that they felt completely ready for. Essentially, you never truly know how prepared you are.

Besides, what's the use in worrying on the day of the exam? There's no time left to go back and revise some more, so there's no point in getting stressed about it once you're in the room. Try and get into the current moment and power through it.

If you're a student at AS level, remember that you've still got the next year to make up for things if you don't do as well as expected. A2 is usually worth more in terms of marks than AS level, so you can certainly make up for it the following year.

Here are some other tips for keeping calm in the exam:

- **Breathing exercises.** If you find yourself getting nervous before exams, or struggle to get to sleep due to exam anxiety, then breathing exercises could be beneficial.

- **Get into the moment.** Just before and during your exam, it can help to go into "exam-mode". By this, we mean blocking off outside distractions and any negativity coming from anywhere. Sometimes, having friends and classmates talk about the possible contents of the exam just before entering can put you off. It might make you feel as if you've missed out on something major, and then cause you to worry once you enter the exam room. Put all of this out of your mind as soon as you enter the room. Once you're in the exam, there's no use fretting about those details.

- **Positive thinking.** This might seem obvious, but thinking positively about the exam and what comes after can be extremely helpful. Some people like to change their mind-set about exams, thinking of it as an opportunity to show off their knowledge, rather than as a painful task that they have to work their way through. Alternatively, focus on what you do know rather than what you don't know, what you can do rather than what you can't do. Once you're in the exam room, there's no point worrying about your weaknesses. Focus on your strengths.

ANSWER THE EASIEST QUESTIONS FIRST

This tip is absolutely key for the tougher exams you come across, since it's an excellent way to use your time in the exam hall effectively.

Say you're about to sit an exam. You sit down and have the examination instructions read out to you. The invigilator instructs you to start your exam, and then you begin. You open the question booklet to find that the first question seems almost impossible. Before you panic, take a flick through the booklet and take a look at some of the other questions. If possible, pick the question that looks the easiest to you and start with that.

This is a good technique for two reasons. Firstly, it's a great boost to your confidence when you're feeling unsure about the exam. There's not much worse in an exam than sitting there, becoming more and more demoralised by a question that you don't think you can answer. Starting with more manageable questions will help you ease into the exam, and hopefully you'll recall some information while doing it.

Sometimes, exams can fit together like a puzzle. At first, it seems impossible. But, once you start to put pieces in (answer the questions), the more difficult bits start to make sense. All of a sudden, you're on a roll of answering questions, and then the tough ones don't seem so bad!

The other reason that this is a good technique, is that it represents a good use of your time. There's no point sitting and staring blankly at a question that you can't solve, when there are others that you could be getting on with. Forget about the tough questions for now, bank as many marks as you can with the easier ones, then go back to the hard ones at the end if you have time. This way, you can secure as many marks as possible. In the worst-case scenario, you won't be able to complete the tough questions, but you'll still have earned a few points for all of the others.

ANSWER THE QUESTION

One of the biggest mistakes that students make throughout their academic lives is failing to answer the question that they've actually been asked. This is particularly the case for essay-based exams such as English Literature, but applies to all of your exams.

DOUBLE-CHECK THE QUESTION

In the next section, we'll be talking about double-checking answers, but it's just as important to double-check the question that you're answering, before you begin to answer it. Say you're doing a maths question:

$$8.93 \times 9.54 = ?$$

Before you start answering the question, take note of everything about it. Where are the decimal points? What operation needs to be performed? Sometimes, people make silly mistakes and misread the question, getting things mixed up.

It's not pleasant finding out that you've answered a question incorrectly just as you get to the end of it, so it pays to look over the question multiple times. In the case of maths questions, it might help to re-write the question in the answer box if there's space. This means you can look back at it quickly, without making any mistakes.

AVOID BLANKING

Have you ever been in a situation where you had something in your head that you were about to say, or about to write, but then completely forgot what it was just before saying or writing it? It can be frustrating in everyday life, but when it happens in an exam it can lead to all kinds of problems. Key details can be forgotten, formulas and tricks may be hard to recall, and sometimes you might just struggle to get off the first page. This is what people refer to as 'blanking'.

Blanking is something that many students worry about, and you've likely heard some horror stories about people who have forgotten everything just as they enter the exam room. However, it doesn't occur as often as you might think, and it doesn't mean you're going to fail your exam.

The best way to prevent blanking is to keep stress to a minimum. This might be easier said than done, but students tend to blank when they haven't had much sleep or have tried

to cram their revision into the day before, or the day of the exam itself. This can cause students to panic, and while they're busy worrying, anything that might have been holding in their short-term memory gets forgotten. We'll cover stress in more detail later in this chapter.

In addition to keeping stress to a minimum, make sure that you aren't revising on the day of your exam, and preferably not the night before, either. In order to retain the information in your revision, you need to commit it to what some people call your 'long-term memory'. It takes time for what you've studied to reach this part of your memory, and things revised in the hours before the exam usually haven't made it there. When revision is being held in the short-term memory, you're generally more likely to forget it, which in turn leads to blanking.

If you find that you've blanked in your exam, here are some tips to keep you calm and help you recover from it as quickly as possible:

TIP 1

Take a few deep breaths before continuing. This is important as you need to stay calm. The more you panic, the less likely you are to remember the information you need. Take a moment to calm down – remember that not performing so well on this exam isn't the end of the world, and that you have the entire paper to remember what you need to know and get back on form.

TIP 2

Look through the question booklet. Sometimes, the wording of a question can jog your memory, or give you a clue of what to write. This can get you started on an answer, which in turn can set off a chain-reaction of memories flooding back, to the point where you remember plenty of information. However, this doesn't always happen; don't rely on this as a replacement for revising over a longer period of time.

TIP 3

Start with an easier question. Some questions require less knowledge than others. If you find yourself blanking in the exam, go onto a question that doesn't need as much precise information as others. Sometimes, a question won't be asking for specific terms or details, but rather an analysis or critical take on the material. These are the questions to do first if you find yourself blanking. This won't work for every kind of exam, however.

TIP 4

Don't attempt any of the larger questions. It might be tempting to just throw caution to the wind and get the toughest or biggest question out of the way. This is usually a bad idea, since these questions contain the most marks. You want to answer these once you've remembered as much as possible, so wait until later in the exam to try them.

TIP 5

It's not the end of the world. If you find yourself running out of time, don't panic. Answer as many questions as you can to secure as many marks as possible. It isn't the end of the world if you don't do so well, and you'll have other exams in which to pick up some marks.

DOUBLE-CHECK YOUR WORK

Everyone makes mistakes. It's almost completely unavoidable, even under relaxed conditions, to create a piece of work that's free of any errors at all. In an exam, you're going to feel a bit rushed, and you're probably going to be working very quickly. This is fine, but remember that you're more likely to make mistakes this way. So, it's important that you go back and check everything you've written. Small, silly errors can cost you big marks, so it's vital to make sure you've fixed anything that could be wrong.

Proofreading can take place at two times during your exam. You can either re-read each of your answers individually after you've completed each one, or you can go back at the end of the exam (if you have time) and check every question in one go. There are benefits and drawbacks to both.

HOW CAN I PREVENT EXAM STRESS?

First of all, remember that exam stress is completely normal for candidates sitting exams. These exams might be very important, and if you're feeling stressed about them it at least shows that you recognise their significance. While stress definitely isn't a good thing, the bright side of it is that you and your body are aware of how important your exams are. Now what's needed is to keep your stress levels down so you can operate at peak performance, and more importantly stay healthy in body and mind!

This section will cover the "dos" and "don'ts" for dealing with exam stress, both during revision and the exams themselves.

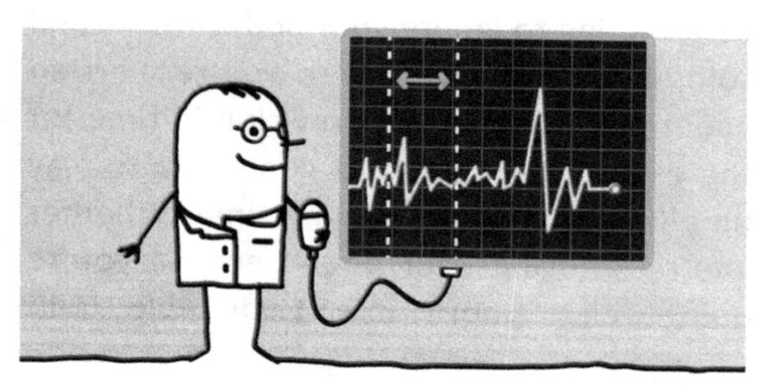

DO...

Start revision early. This might seem obvious by now, but starting your revision earlier in the year is one of the best ways to avoid stress. The more time you have, the less you need to do each day. This gives you more free time, and also allows you to make use of extra time to do other revision activities such as practice papers.

Have a countdown to the end of your exams. Buy a calendar and make note of all your exam dates. Tick days off as they go by, and stay focused on the end. Staying aware of the end point of your exams will remind you that there's life after your exams. There is light at the end of the tunnel.

Listen to your body. At times, you might feel like an unstoppable machine, speeding through revision. During this period, it can be tempting to ignore your bodily needs and soldier on. Likewise, when you're worried about not finishing your revision in time for the exam, it seems like a good idea to stay up all night to make up lost time. Whether you're ignoring your body because you're doing well or poorly, it isn't advisable to do so. You can't function properly without food, water and sleep, so remember to take the breaks in your revision to do these things. That way, when you come back to revising, your study sessions will be more valuable because you're able to focus harder.

Forget about the exam once it's over. It's likely that you'll have more than one exam. You might even have multiple exams on consecutive days, or even on the same day. So, it's important not to linger on an exam once you've finished it. As soon as the exam ends, you have permission to forget about it entirely. Try and avoid talking to others about details of the exam, because it might give you second thoughts about what you wrote in yours. There's no use worrying now since there's no way of changing what you've written. Stay confident and move onto the next exam.

Ask others for support. No person is an island, and everyone occasionally needs someone else to help them through tough times. Exams can be difficult, and a lot of pressure is put on candidates taking exams, especially academic ones such as GCSE and A-Level. When the going gets tough, don't be afraid to talk to your friends and family. Find people you trust and talk to them about your worries. Sometimes, just talking about things can make you feel calmer, even if you don't figure out any solutions. More often than not, your worries will be amplified by the general worry of exams, and so talking through your problems and rationalising them can be a form of therapy. You might find that your worries are just the result of paranoia, and aren't grounded in reality.

DON'T...

Rely on online forums. The internet can be an excellent place to find information and techniques for studying. You have access to plenty of specific advice on a range of subjects, and this can supplement your work in the classroom and your revision at home. However, not all resources are useful, and not all environments on the internet are good for your wellbeing. Some exam-focused chatrooms and forums can do more harm than good. You may come across people who are arrogant about the work that they've done, trying to make you feel worse about your studies as a result. Make use of the internet when it comes to your exams, but try not to linger in places that won't make you feel better about your own studies.

Set goals you can't meet. Always remember that there's only so much that you can do each day when it comes to revision. If you've put together a revision timetable then this shouldn't be a problem, but double-check how much work you've allotted for each day. During the revision period, take note of how much you're doing each day, and adjust your timetable based on this. For example, if you're finding that 10 topics is far too many, try reducing it to 7 or 8. Likewise, if you're able to do loads more than 5, experiment and see how many topics you get through in one day. The aim of this is to finish each day satisfied that you did everything you can, and that everything is completed. This should work towards preventing exam stress.

Panic about your exam timetable. Occasionally, you might not meet all of your goals for the day. While this isn't a good thing, you need to remember that you always have the next day to cover what you failed to achieve the day before. At the end of your revision for the day, you should try and put yourself in the mind-set that everything is fine – meaning that you can relax and get some quality sleep.

CONCLUSION

You've now reached the end of *Studying with Dyslexia*. Hopefully it's provided some helpful tips that you can employ in your studies to help reduce the stress surrounding reading, writing, and taking exams. Aiming to keep calm and stress-free is incredibly important for every student, so make sure to look after yourself and always ask for help if you need it.

As well as this, be sure to seek the support you're entitled to as a dyslexic student. If you're at school or university, make sure that you talk to a teacher or advisor who has the necessary power to arrange extra time and other resources available to you to further your education.

A FEW FINAL WORDS...

For any test, it is helpful to keep the following in mind...

The Three 'P's

1. Preparation. Preparation is key to passing any test; you won't be doing yourself any favours by not taking the time to prepare. Many fail their tests because they did not know what to expect or did not know what their own weaknesses were. Take the time to go over any areas you may have struggled with. By doing this, you will become familiar with how you will perform on the day of the test.

2. Perseverance. If you set your sights on a goal and stick to it, you are more likely to succeed. Obstacles and setbacks are common when trying to achieve something great, and you shouldn't shy away from them. Instead, face the tougher parts of the test, even if you feel defeated. If you need to, take a break from your work to relax and then return with renewed vigour. If you fail the test, take the time to consider why you failed, gather your strength and try again.

3. Performance. How well you perform will be the result of your preparation and perseverance. Remember to relax when taking the test and try not to panic. Believe in your own abilities, practise as much as you can, and motivate yourself constantly. Nothing is gained without hard work and determination, and this applies to how you perform on the day of the test.

We wish you the best of luck in all of your future endeavours!

Rapid Study Skills for Students Series

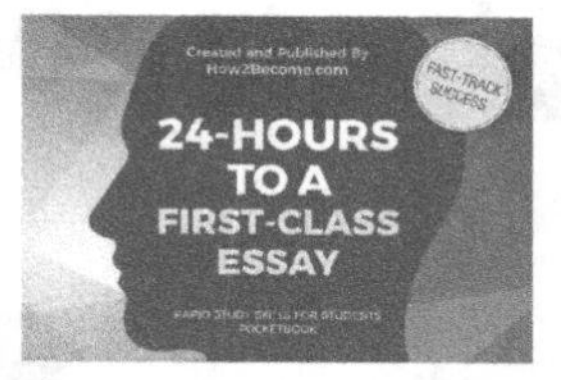

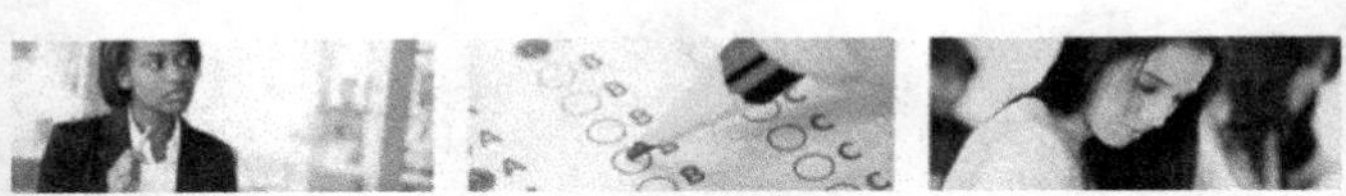

CPSIA information can be obtained
at www.ICGtesting.com
Printed in the USA
BVHW081317200123
656715BV00013B/1069

9 781912 370146